Cancún

The Delaplaine 2021 Long Weekend Guide

Andrew Delaplaine

**NO BUSINESS HAS PAID A SINGLE PENNY OR GIVEN *ANYTHING*
TO BE INCLUDED IN THIS BOOK.**

GET 3 *FREE* NOVELS
Like political thrillers?
See next page to download 3 FREE page-turning
novels—no strings attached.

Senior Editors
Renee & Sophie Delaplaine
Copyright Gramercy Park Press
All rights reserved

Gramercy Park Press
New York London Paris

WANT 3 FREE THRILLERS?

Why, of course you do!

If you like these writers--
Vince Flynn, Brad Thor, Tom Clancy, James Patterson, David Baldacci, John Grisham, Brad Meltzer, Daniel Silva, Don DeLillo
If you like these TV series –
House of Cards, Scandal, West Wing, The Good Wife, Madam Secretary, Designated Survivor

> You'll love the **unputdownable** series about Jack Houston St. Clair, with political intrigue, romance, and loads of action and suspense.

Besides writing travel books, I've written political thrillers for many years that have delighted hundreds of thousands of readers. I want to introduce you to my work!
Send me an email and I'll send you a link where you can download the first 3 books in my bestselling series, **absolutely FREE.**

Mention **this book** when you email me.

andrewdelaplaine@mac.com

**The Delaplaine
Long Weekend Guide**

TABLE OF CONTENTS

**Chapter 1
FIRST THINGS FIRST – 5**
Why Cancún?
Transportation & Tips for Getting Around
Information

**Chapter 2
LODGING – 11**
Budget – Mid-Range - Luxury

**Chapter 3
RESTAURANTS – 31**
Budget – Mid-Range - Pricey

**Chapter 4
NIGHTLIFE – 51**

**Chapter 5
ATTRACTIONS – 58**
Water Sports

**Chapter 6
SHOPPING & SERVICES – 70**

INDEX – 73

Other Books by the Same Author – 76

Chapter 1
FIRST THINGS FIRST

Why Cancún?

Being world travelers, we knew the reputation of Cancún. We knew that Cancún is the Mecca of spring breakers and pasty Americans desperately seeking a weekend respite from biting winters. So it was with trepidation that, years ago, we first stepped foot on that hotel-covered sandbar. We dutifully wiggled into our bathing suits, slathered ourselves in sunblock, and walked out onto the beach. And then we finally understood it – we got why millions of people every year flock to this far corner of the Yucatán Peninsula. *Cancún has got a world-class beach.*

We have been on many beaches around the world. And none of them are quite as magical as the one in Cancún. The sun is strong, but a constant gentle breeze keeps one comfortable. On first sight, you will not believe the color of the water you're looking at actually exists in nature. It really is a clear, bright turquoise. Waves lap gently on fine sand the color of cappuccino. The slope is very gradual, so you can head far into the water and still touch the bottom. And the temperature of the water is perfect year-round.

But there is more. There is something else about this beach that we just can't put our finger on. There is an idyllic serenity the likes of which we have never encountered before or since. Here we find an eclectic mix of all kinds, local and tourist. Here we find an elderly couple holding hands staring at the sea, a few yards from a group of beer-chugging frat boys. And all the people have a blissed-out, faraway smile on their faces. Yes, there is something magical about the beach in Cancún.

Mind you, Cancún is a tourist town. By far, the local industry is tourism, and most of what goes on in Cancún is designed to separate you from what you have in your wallet. If you are looking to get to know the culture and people the Yucatán Peninsula, Cancún is not the place for you. It is for good reason that Yucatecans call Cancún "Gringolandia." If you want to experience the true culture of the area, you will have to go to the ancient city of nearby Mérida.

Transportation & Tips for Getting Around

AIRPORT & TAXIS

Cancún Airport can be an unnerving and high-pressure experience. As soon as you disembark, you'll encounter dozens of pushy vendors representing various businesses, all trying to sell you (and sell you *hard*) a timeshare or a tour, or even just a taxi ride. The taxi people and cabbies can be very pushy. Take my advice and do yourself a favor—book yourself a pickup service before you arrive. They will meet you as you arrive and usher you through the craziness to your waiting van. You'll be at your hotel before you know it. (Many hotels offer free transfers—check to be sure.)

Rates from the airport run up to $60 one way, 20-mile trip to the Zona Hotelera (Hotel Zone). They only charge you half when you go the other way.

SHUTTLE SERVICE

A cheaper shuttle service is operated by Hertz and the Green Line. It runs every half hour. Buy your ticket when you get here.

BUS SERVICE

There's bus service from the airport into Cancun that runs just a few dollars.

RENTING A CAR

Renting a car is a great way to explore the many opportunities the Yucatán Peninsula has to offer. I recommend reserving your car ahead of time. When renting your car, it is ***very important*** that you specifically request insurance equal to the value of the car. It is not made clear when you pick it up, but you are personally responsible for any damage to the car. Upon return you are at the mercy of the staff for any scratch, so be very aware of the condition of the vehicle when you get it and make sure each ding and dent is noted in the rental agreement before you drive away. It's better to arrange your rental before you leave on your trip to be assured you get a car. All the major car rental firms are represented here.

INFORMATION

CANCUN MUNICIPAL TOURISM OFFICE
Corner of Avenida Nader & Avenida Cobá: 998-887-3379. Open weekdays.

CANCUN CONVENTION BUREAU
www.cancun.travel (no .com after travel)

GENERAL INFORMATION
www.cancun.com
www.cancuntips.com

Chapter 2
LODGINGS

Timeshares

Budget - Cuidad Cancun (Downtown)

Budget - Isla Cancun (Beach-Zona Hotelera)
Moderate – Isla Cancun (Beach-Zona Hotelera)
Luxury – Isla Cancun (Beach-Zona Hotelera)

TIMESHARES

A word about timeshares. Many hotels and resorts in Cancún are associated with timeshare programs. Visitors are often invited to a timeshare presentation in return for a complimentary gift, such as a free meal. We urge you to attend the presentation ONLY IF YOU ARE SINCERELY INTERESTED IN A TIMESHARE. We have been to more timeshare presentations than we care to think about and we can assure you the complimentary gift is never worth the inconvenience. Sales techniques are tricky and often high-pressure, and more than one innocent vacationer has awakened the next day with a bad case of buyer's remorse. So if you are approached with a timeshare invitation, we urge you to firmly say NO and walk away. These people (they're under a lot of pressure themselves because they only get paid after they fleece you) do not give a damn about you, and you can't—*repeat, CAN'T*—hurt their feelings. So do not give them the time of day.

Budget - Cuidad Cancun (Downtown)

SOL Y LUNA
Calle Alcatraces 33, Parque Las Palapas, Lote 33 Mz. 9 SM 22, Quintana Roo,
Cancun: 52-998-887-5579
http://caribya.com/cancun/sol.y.luna/
 Situated on the floors above a tapas place you'll find this 10-room inn. Nothing fancy, but basic and nice. Perfect for exploring downtown where most of the locals live. A nice enough little eatery is located on premises, El Rincón del Vino.

XBALAMQUÉ
Av. Yaxchilán 31, Sm. 22, Mz. 17, Quintana Roo,
Cancun: 52-998-193-2720
www.xbalamque.com
This place is a real find. The furnishings are very much reflective of the countryside, with great tilework. They've tried to make the whole place look very Mayan, with yard after yard of murals, paintings and sculptures done in that style. All the furniture is very rough-hewn (but you'll wish you had a few pieces when you get back home.) There's a refreshingly calming waterfall in the pool area. There's a beautifully quaint courtyard and they have a few junior suites. (Food in the Adelita restaurant is good, too, and those cool local beers are great.)

Budget - Isla Cancun (Beach-Zona Hotelera)

GRAND ROYAL LAGOON
Calle Quetzal No. 8-A | Boulevard Kukulcán Km 7.5, 52-998-883-2749
https://bighotels.org/product/grand-royal-lagoon/
If you want to stay in the Hotel Zone on a budget, then this is the place for you. It is interestingly located on the back side of the sandbar on the lagoon, so don't expect to walk out your door onto the beach. But the beach is in walking distance, and all beachfront is common property in Mexico, so feel free to use another hotel's beach. It is also a short walk to shopping and the big clubs the zone is known for. The rooms are basic and clean; the showers are big with plenty of hot water and good pressure. Most rooms have kitchenettes. We recommend upgrading to a balcony for $10. The breakfast is tasty.

HOTEL DEL SOL
Av. Lopez Portillo Mz 2Lt 1A SM85, Puerto Juarez, Mexico: 52-998-880-3693
www.hotel-del-sol.cancunhotelmexico.net/en
This hotel is not in Cancún proper, it is in Puerto Juarez, about eight kilometers north of Cancún, so it is a bit far from the all the attractions of the city and the Hotel/Beach Zone. It is, however, perfectly located forsea ad excursions to Isla de Mujeres, with the ferry right across the street. The hotel has excellent views of the ocean, but there is no serviceable beach for miles, and there is no pool. The rooms are very clean and the service efficient.

HOTEL EL REY DEL CARIBE
Av. Uxmal 24 | Corner of Uxmal and Nader, Cancún 77500, Mexico: 52-998-884-2028
www.reycaribe.com
This lovely hotel can be appropriately described as an oasis. It is located in downtown Cancún, but once you've entered the compound you feel as though you've entered another world. The gardens are simply wonderful. You'll enjoy the hammocks by the pool. This is an eco-conscious hotel, so you'll appreciate all the green touches. The rooms are big, and on the upper floors include a kitchenette.

HOTEL RAMADA CANCÚN CITY
Avenida Yaxchilan 41, Cancún 77500, Mexico: 52-998-881-7870/ 800-640-7473
www.ramadacancun.com
Another good, clean basic hotel. It is located in the city proper, but they have a free shuttle to the Beach /Hotel Zone. There are a lot of good restaurants in the area, but also consider the hotel restaurant; it is

surprisingly good. The staff is courteous and professional.

TERRACARIBE HOTEL
Av Lopez Portillo 70 | Esquina Av. Bonampak, Cancún 77500, Mexico: 52 998 211 3015, 1-800-837-7222
https://terracaribehotelboutique.com-cancun.com/
This place likes to bill itself as a boutique hotel. It's not a boutique hotel, it's just a plain no-frills hotel. But it is a clean hotel with good service. The staff here are very friendly. The downside is the location, it is in the city and the neighborhood is a little rustic. The restaurant food is tasty, and the bar offers good drinks and great service. All in all, a great value.

SOTAVENTO HOTEL AND YACHT CLUB
Blv. Kukulkan km 4 Zona Hotelera | Lote D.8.3 Calle Pescador, Cancún 77500, Mexico: 52-998-884-1540
http://www.hotelsotavento.info/
Located on the northern edge of the Beach/Hotel Zone across the street from the beach hotels, and overlooking the lagoon. It is a basic no frills hotel with a nice pool and garden area.

SUITES GABY HOTEL
Av. Sunyaxche Lote 46 y 47 | Mza 2 Supermanzana 25 CP, Cancún 77509, Mexico: 52-998-887-8037
https://www.suitesgaby.com.mx/index
A decent basic hotel in the center of Cancún. The rooms are clean with internet available. It is conveniently located near the bus station and also quite close to the tourist market.

Moderate – Isla Cancun (Beach-Zona Hotelera)

ALL RITMO RESORT & WATERPARK
Km 1.5 Carretera a Punta Juarez-Punta Sam, Cancún 77500, Mexico: 52 81 5350 3400/ 877-734-3186
www.allritmocancun.com

As you can tell from the name, this is a very kid-friendly resort. But it is also lots of fun for adults. The staff is very keyed in to entertaining and offering a good time. There are all sorts of activities offered, such as the waterpark, games, snorkeling, boating and surprisingly good Vegas-style shows in the evening. The rooms are very large and well maintained. The hotel is located off the tourist strip, up north a bit in Puerto Juarez, and is conveniently located near the ferry to Isla Mujeres.

AVALON BACCARA
Blvd. Kukulcan Km 11.5 | Zona
Hotelera, Cancún 77500, Mexico:
998-881-3900/ 1-800-507-1239
www.hotelavalonbaccaracancun.com
The Avalon Baccara, is, put simply, an excellent hotel. It is quiet and intimate. There are only about 30 rooms in the hotel. The setting is peaceful and out of the way. The staff, from the management to the maids, is consistent in the superior service they offer. The rooms are spotless and relaxing, each one featuring a balcony with Jacuzzi. The grounds are well-kept, from the colorful pool to the groomed beach. The food is delicious. We can't recommend enough the Avalon Baccara.

BEL AIR COLLECTION RESORT & SPA
Boulevard Kukulcan Km. 20.5 Hotel
Zone, Cancún 77500, Mexico:
52-800-400-2040/01 800 523 2223
www.belaircancun.com
There is good and bad at the Bel Air. Let's get the bad out of the way. The building is old and it has old building problems. Air conditioning problems is a constant battle for the maintenance staff. Now the good -- the staff is very efficient and courteous. The common areas are comfortable and stylish. Most of the common areas are open air and accented by billowing white curtains. The food is quite good, particularly the Italian restaurant, Ciao Mexico. We also recommend the spa… a massage on the beach in

the evening is just the thing before hitting the nightclubs or puttering off to bed.

KRYSTAL GRAND PUNTA CANCUN
Blvd Kukulcan Km 8.5, Hotel Zone, Cancún 77500, Mexico:
998-891-5555
www.krystal-hotels.com
The building is a bit dated, but is well-maintained. The lobby tends to get a bit warm, but the rooms have excellent AC. The hotel is tall, so the upper floors have excellent views no matter what side you are one. Location is everything, and the Krystal has excellent location. The hotel sits in a quiet cul-de-sac just next to the nightclub zone and restaurants. It also boasts one of the best sections of beach, where the water is most calm.

LE BLANC SPA
Blvd. Kukulkan Km. 10, Cancún, 888-702-0913
www.leblancsparesort.com
An adults-only beach all-inclusive resort offers 260 rooms with balconies featuring great ocean or lagoon views – many with sitting areas and whirlpool tubs. Amenities include: flat-screen LED TVs, Bvlgari bath amenities, 24-hour butler services, complimentary Wi-Fi, complimentary breakfast and parking. Hotel facilities include: 4 on-site dining options, 6 bars, fitness center, golf course, outdoor pools, and the **Blanc Spa** (with those long white curtains billowing in the breeze, just like in the movies). Beach access. AAA Five Diamond Award.

MARRIOTT CASAMAGNA CANCÚN RESORT
Blvd Kukulcan, Retorno Chac L-41 | Zona Hotelera, Cancún 77500, Mexico: 52-998-881-2000
www.marriott.com
The Marriott offers everything you would expect from a resort hotel. Room service is quick. The rooms are large and clean. We recommend you spring for an ocean view. Also, when booking your room, get the package that includes the breakfast buffet. Trust us, you'll be glad you did. The CasaMagna breakfast buffet is the stuff of legends.

NIZUC RESORT & SPA
Blvd Kukulkan Mz 59 Lote 1-01 Km 21.26, Cancun, +52 998 891 5700
www.nizuc.com
An ideal resort for golf lovers, beachfront resort is located right next to a golf course. Though this is a large resort (about 30 acres), it feels much more intimate because of the mangroves surrounding the place. There's a barrier reef not far from the shore, so explore that when you go snorkeling. This resort offers 274 soundproofed rooms with high ceilings. The garden villas offer more privacy, if that's what you're looking for. The penthouse suites have "outdoor living rooms." Amenities include: complimentary Wi-Fi, iPod docks, flat-screen TVs, Nespresso machines and minibars. Resort facilities include: 6 restaurants (including **Terra Nostra**, with an Italian motif and the modern Mexican spot **Ramona**), 2 lounge bars, 2 pools, tennis courts, a full-service spa, and a gym. Family friendly facility.

Conveniently located near attractions like the Playa Delfines beach and the Interactive Aquarium.

OMNI CANCÚN HOTEL
Blvd Kukulcan km 16.5, Hotel
Zone, Cancún 77500, Mexico: 52-998-881-0600
www.omnihotels.com
The Omni is still a good hotel, but it may be a bit on the old side. The beds are very comfortable, but the rooms are small and the bathrooms are smaller.
You'll get great service from the staff, particularly the beach staff. The food is not very impressive, so head out when dining.

TEMPTATION RESORT SPA CANCÚN
Blvd. Kukulcan km 3.5 | Zona Hotelera/ Hotel
Zone, Cancún 77500, Mexico: 52-998-848-7900/
877-485-8367
https://www.temptation-experience.com/
Temptation is an all-inclusive adults-only resort, which means you can eat and/or drink to your heart's content, and you can probably find someone to do it with you. There is a definite party atmosphere.

There are lots of ways to meet people, with activities going on round the clock. It has a reputation as a bit of a swingers' hotel. But you don't have to be a horny single to enjoy the resort. There is a "sexy" pool and there is a "quiet" pool. Rooms are clean, staff is on the ball, and the food is pretty good. We recommend The Wok restaurant.

WESTIN LAGUNAMAR CANCÚN
Km 12.5 Blvd Kukulcan | Zona Hotelera, PO Box 834 Apdo., Cancún 77500, Mexico: 52-998-891-4200
www.marriott.com/hotels
This is a timeshare resort. They are going to want you to listen to their sales pitch, which we recommend you avoid unless you really are interested. The hotel facilities are top notch. All the suites have wifi, balconies, washer/dryers, and kitchens stocked with some basics. If cooking your own food is not your idea of a vacation, the hotel is in walking distance of some very excellent restaurants, which the hotel staff will happily direct you to. They will also help you with the myriad of activities offered at the resort. The grounds are beautiful, and their pool and fountain system is spectacular.

Luxury – Isla Cancun (Beach-Zona Hotelera)

EXCELLENCE RIVIERA
Carretera Federal 307 Chetumal, Puerto Juarez | Manzana 7, Lote 1, S.M. 11, Puerto Morelos 77580, Mexico: 52-998-872-8500, 1-866-540-2585
www.excellence-resorts.com

The Excellence is an all-inclusive resort located in Puerto Morelos, just south of Cancún. The staff really stresses the notion that you are home. That is if your home has hundreds of servants running around anticipating your every wish. And should your wish be a drink, then you are in the right spot. The bar staff is very knowledgeable, and they serve only quality brands. If you don't care for alcohol, we highly recommend the cucumber lemonade. Foodwise there are 8 on site restaurants to choose from. We recommend the tepanyaki. Room service is quick and available 24 hours a day.

FIESTA AMERICANA GRAND CORAL BEACH RESORT & SPA
Blvd Kukulcan Km 9.5 Lote 6 | Zona Hotelera, Cancún 77500, Mexico:
998-881-3200, 1-800-343-7821
www.fiestamericanagrand.com
Just what you'd expect from a five star hotel. The staff is courteous and always there with anything you need. The rooms are well-designed. Beds are luxurious with lots of comfy pillows. The bathrooms are almost entire suites in themselves. The food in the restaurants is pricey, but well worth it. Despite the name, this is not a party hotel – things quiet down after midnight, but it is within stumbling distance of the nightclubs, if that's your thing.

RITZ-CARLTON
Retorno del Rey 36 | Zona Hotelera, Quintana Roo, Cancún 77500, Mexico: 52-998-881-0808
www.ritzcarlton.com

As one would expect from the Ritz-Carlton, this is a sumptuously laid out resort. The building and the grounds are beautiful. All that can be said of the rooms is they are perfect. The pool areas are luxurious and relaxing. The staff is always on the lookout for a way to make you more comfortable. The fitness area features state of the art equipment, and there is bottled water and fresh towels at every station. The beach, of course, is beautiful, relaxing and perfectly groomed. If you plan on using a cabana at the beach, reserve it ahead of time. Upgrading to the hotel's Club Level will get you ever more stellar services and luxury, and all food, drinks and alcohol are included. If you are a fan of the Ritz's exceptional food, which can be quite pricey, you can save considerably by upgrading.

RIU PALACE LAS AMERICAS
Blvd Kukulcan, Km 8.5, Manzana 50 | Lote 4, Zona Hotelera, Cancún 77500, Mexico: 52-998-891-4300/ 888-666-8816
www.riu.com

All-inclusive resort on the Hotel-zone. The staff is friendly. The building is a bit old, and by today's standards, the rooms are small. Also, the walls are rather thin, and you had better hope for a quiet neighbor. That said, the staff is working constantly to keep the grounds in good condition. The food is pretty good, and there's lots of top-shelf booze. 24 hour room service is also a nice touch.

LIVE AQUA ALL-INCLUSIVE
Boulevard Kukulcan Km. 12.5 Zona Hotelera, Cancún 77500, Mexico: 52-998-881-7600/ 800-343-7821
www.feel-aqua.com
The building here is very beautiful and well designed, there is a light and airy feel to the place. Walking in to the lobby for the first time is an impressive sight. The pools are ubiquitous; you could swim in a different pool every day, and still not hit them all in a week. And in that week you will never see or hear a

child… they are simply not allowed. The rooms are nice … great if you upgrade to a suite. The staff is friendly. Drinks can be a bit weak, so feel free to order an extra shot. We found the food at Live Aqua to be a bit weak also. Of the restaurant options, the best is MB.

MOON PALACE GOLF & SPA RESORT
Carretera Federal 307 Km
340, Cancún 77500, Mexico: 52-998-881-6000/ 800-986-5632
www.moonpalacecancun.com
All-inclusive. The resort is huge, so take advantage of the many golf carts. All rooms have a balcony. Obviously one of the big draws of this place are the golf courses, which have been installed with a respect for the local environment, so while you're teeing off, you might get a chance to see a crocodile.

SUN PALACE
Blvd. Kukulcan KM. 20 | Zona
Hotelera, Cancún 77500, Mexico: 800-986-5632
www.palaceresorts.com
Devoted guests tend to come back to the Sun Palace year after year. The staff is warm and friendly and very accommodating. We recommend you upgrade to the concierge level; the extra amenities and superior room make it well worth it. All the rooms in the hotel are large and comfortable. Our only issue is the toilets in the bathrooms could stand to have some privacy walls if you are going to be sharing the bathroom.

ZOETRY PARAISO DE LA BONITA
Carretera Cancún-Chetumal km 328, Puerto Morelos 77580, Mexico: 52-998-872-8300
www.zoetryresorts.com

The Zoetry is not actually in Cancún, but in Puerto Morelos, a few minutes south, but is about the same distance from the airport. Speaking of airport, one very nice feature is the hotel will pick you up, so you don't have to worry about taxis. Being away from the tourist zone of Cancún, the resort feels secluded and peaceful. When you get to your room you'll find a bottle of champagne and a bottle of tequila… live it up. The food here is healthy and delicious, with many dishes featuring organic ingredients.

THE ROYAL CANCÚN
Kukulkan Km 11.5 Hotel
Kukulcan Km. 4.5 Lotes C2 & C2A, Zona Hotelera, 77500 Cancún, QROO, Mexico, 52 800 888 7744
www.royalresorts.com

This is an excellent all-inclusive resort and the flagship of Real Resorts. First class service through and through. The rooms are fantastic. Finicky sleepers will love the beds and appreciate the "Pillow Menu." Each room has dispensers of call-brand whiskey, vodka, rum and tequila. You are never at a want for anything. There is a variety of different restaurants in the hotel, most notable is the Asiana. The hotel buffet is a little ho-hum. The beach is always impeccably groomed. And for those of you who can't stand to be out of touch, there is a strong wifi signal everywhere.

Chapter 3
RESTAURANTS

Budget

100% NATURAL
Juices, Sandwiches, Lunch, Healthy, Vegetarian, Vegan
Av. Sunyaxche lote 62, Supermanzana 25, Mza. 6 (Col. Centro), Cancún, Quintana Roo 77500, Mexico: 52-998-884-0102
www.100natural.com.mx
100% Natural is a restaurant chain that is happily taking Mexico by storm. The food offered is free of

preservatives and artificial flavors and colorings. For breakfast, lunch and dinner, healthy fare is the theme. The juice bar offers fresh made juices from local fruits and veggies. The delicious whole-wheat bread is baked fresh on-site, so try one of their tasty sandwiches. We recommend the veggie burger.

CALYPSO'S GRILL AND MEXICAN FOOD
Seafood, Mexican
Kukulcan Ave. km 8.5 next to Cancun Center, Cancún 77500, Mexico:
52 998-883-1244 / 52 998-214-5393
www.calypsoscancunrestaurant.com
WEBSITE DOWN AT PRESSTIME
Calypso's is a good basic no-frills restaurant in the Hotel Zone across from the Fiesta Americana. The owner, Felipe, is a character, and loves goofing around with his customers. The Mexican food is so-

so. The Seafood is what we recommend. It's good eating, and a great value. The plate of Lobster Tails is our favorite item. And don't miss the house tequila.

RESTAURANTE LE NATURA
Mexican, Health, Vegetarian, Seafood
Boulevard Kukulcan km 9.5 | Zona Hotelera, Cancún 77500, Mexico:
52 998-883-0585
www.restaurantenatura.com
Here is a great way to start your day in the Hotel Zone. This inexpensive little eatery is right across the

street from Señor Frog's. They have a large variety of fruit juices and smoothies they offer, including some tasty options you've probably never had. Their breakfast plates, such as the Juevos Rancheros, are big and tasty. Or if you're into healthier fare you can get the fruit platter, which is huge. And you can get your breakfast served at any time of the day, which is a feature we always like. They don't stop at breakfast. There is a good selection of tasty dishes for both vegetarians and carnivores.

THE SURFIN BURRITO
Mexican
Kukulcan Blvd. Km 9.5, Cancún, Mexico: 52-998-883-0083
https://www.facebook.com/thesurfinburrito/info?tab=overview

Absolutely the best burrito you will find in Cancún. It's just a little hut with some counters and stools, but it has great atmosphere. You make your selections on an order slip, and they build it for you... Hot and Huge. The tacos are good, but the burritos steal the show. The smoothies are good too, and big. If you prefer your drinks with a kick, they have a bar as well. You might miss it, so remember it is right across the street from Sr. Frog's next to the OXXO. They are open 24 hours and they deliver to the hotel zone.

LA TRANQUITA GRILL AND BAR
Pizza, Burgers, Steaks, Pastas
Ave. Kabah Mz1. Smz 13. Lote 22. Plaza Zona Zentro, Cancún 77500, Mexico:
998-802-1841
www.latranquita.com
This little gem is located away from the tourist zone in Cancún proper. It's a bit out of the way, so have good directions or take a taxi. But once you've gotten there you'll be glad you did. There is something for everyone at La Tranquita, and it's all good. It's better than good. Pizzas, burgers, steaks, pastas, everything is delicious. The friendly staff helmed by Manager Eric, who is always circulating making sure his guests are enjoying their meal. The space is warm and relaxing, and spotlessly clean. Before you leave – and you won't want to leave – have the corn cake for dessert.

TRATTORIA LA VENEZIANA DA BERTILLA
Italian, Pasta, Pizza
Tulipanes n 9 SM 22 MZ 2, Cancún 77500, Mexico:
998-884-8475
https://www.facebook.com/Trattoria-la-veneziana Cancun-Mexico-61880822973/
You can't get more authentic Italian. This is a family run restaurant downtown. Bertilla, Luciano and Sergio moved here from Italy five years ago, and have been drawing devoted customers since. The open-air dining is on a pedestrian street next to popular Parque de las Palapas Park. The Pizzas are real authentic Italian Pizzas… thin, thin crusts and lots of flavor. All their pastas are perfect of course, but we want to rave about the Gnocchi. If you ask us, an Italian Restaurant lives or dies on its Gnocchi. And this trattoria lives, lives, lives!

Mid-Range

BACOLI TRATORIA
Blvd. Kulkukan, Km 17. Retorno Gucumatz,
52 998 283 3800
https://hotelesemporio.com
CUISINE: Italian
DRINKS: Full Bar
SERVING: Dinner
PRICE RANGE: $$
NEIGHBORHOOD: Quintana Roo
Located in Emporio Hotel & Resort, this eatery offers a creative menu of handmade Italian fare and pizzas prepared in a stone oven. Favorites: Calamari and Lasagna. Nice wine list.

ELEFANTA INDIAN CUISINE
Indian
Blvd. Kukulcan Km. 12.5 Zona Hotelera, Plaza La Isla, Cancún 77500, Mexico: 52-998-176-8070
www.elefanta.com.mx
 Elefanta Indian is adjacent to Elefanta Thai, so whichever is your pleasure. The ambiance is superb; one feels transported to a bamboo paradise, overlooking an idyllic lagoon at sunset. The food is delicious. We love curry, and here it is made perfectly. Be advised that the pricing structure is such that you might feel nickel and dimed, and one is charged extra for such things as Rice and Naan.

FRED'S HOUSE & SEAFOOD
Seafood
Kukulkan Kilometro 14.5, Across From JW Marriott Hotel, Cancún 77500, Mexico: 52-998-840-6466
https://fredshouserestaurant.com/
This is a seafood restaurant, so have the seafood. The kitchen perfectly prepares and presents fish. We have many favorites here. The house Seafood Platter features a nice assortment of their best items. Start with the Shrimp Ceviche. The Fresh Lobster, of course, is a feast. And we also like the octopus, which comes drenched in butter. We're very impressed with the kid-friendly atmosphere here. They even have an activity room for kids, complete with video games. And while the kids are gone, have one of Fred's Mojitos.

LA HABICHUELA DOWNTOWN
Seafood, Steaks, Fusion

Margaritas # 25 | Parque de las
Palapas, Cancún 77500, Mexico: 52-998-884-3158
www.lahabichuela.com
Located next to beautiful Parque de la Palapas Park in downtown Cancún, La Habichuela is a favorite with locals and tourists alike; so we recommend you make reservations. The Mayan décor is really well done, and both the dining room and the garden are nice settings, but for a romantic touch, we like the garden. The service staff is well-trained and quite efficient. The food is delicious. We really like the Caesar Salad made tableside – they have lots of nice touches like that. Their signature dish, the Cocobichuela, a lobster and shrimp curry served in a coconut shell, is very popular. And we recommend ending the night with a Mayan Coffee.

LABNA
Yucatecan
Margaritas 29, Next to Parque Las Palapas,
Cancún 77500, Mexico: 52-998-892-3056
www.restaurantelabna.com/
 While in Cancún, we recommend that you get off the beach and get to know a little of the local culture. Labna is a quaint local place in downtown that offers just that. The food and flavorings are that of the Mayan and Yucatecan culture. Be prepared for something different, and you can trust me—it's good. The Pumpkin Seed Spread they bring out is delicious, and we find ourselves filling up on that. But leave room for the real food. For a nice sampling of their dishes, get the Yucatan Trip. We highly recommend the Lime Soup. Our favorite entrée is the Pibil

Chicken. Also high on our list is the Cactus Salad and the Chaya Drink.

LOCANDA PAOLO
Italian, Seafood, Fusion
Bonampak Avenue 145 – Corner Jurel Street,
Cancún, Mexico: 52-998-887-2627
www.locandapaolo.com
Eating at Locanda Paolo is a treat we highly recommend to anyone. The whole event is a thrill for the senses. The décor is modern and trendy, but not cold. All customers are treated like VIPs by the attentive staff, led by the owner, Paolo, who is very hands-on. The menu is full of interesting and creative dishes that delight the palate. We'd like to know where they get their prosciutto from, because it is amazing. And we're always happy to find a restaurant that makes a good authentic Cream Puff!

MAKI TACO
Blvd. Kukulcan, 52 998 848 7500
https://oasishoteles.com/en/restaurants/maki-taco
CUISINE: Mexican/Japanese/Sushi
DRINKS: Full Bar
SERVING: Dinner, Closed Mon & Tues.
PRICE RANGE: $$$
NEIGHBORHOOD: Quintana Roo
Upscale hotel eatery offering a creative menu of a variety of cuisines. Excellent sushi. Favorites: Beef teriyaki and Cold calamari with mole sauce. Impressive tequila selection.

SAVIO'S BISTRO BY LA DOLCE
Italian
km 15 Zona Hotelera | Across from the Gran Meliá Hotel, Cancún, Mexico:
52-998-884-3393
www.cancunitalianrestaurant.com
Located in the Hotel Zone, Savio's is the kind of place you try once, and then you eat there several times a week. The ambience is relaxed with dining indoors and out. The staff is friendly and efficient. All their food is consistently high quality and delicious. We will name a few of our favorites: Eggplant Parmesan, Veal Scallopini, Lasagna

Bollognaise, Calamari. The kitchen accommodates special needs and requests.

Pricey

BLACK HOLE
Grand Oasis Sens Blvd. Kukulkan Km 19.5,
52 998 891 5000
https://oasishoteles.com/es/restaurantes/black-hole
CUISINE: International
DRINKS: Full Bar
SERVING: Dinner, Closed Sundays
PRICE RANGE: $$$$
NEIGHBORHOOD: Quintana Roo
Located at The Pyramid at Grand Oasis, this eatery offers a unique dining experience. Food is served amongst performances. This is a 20+ course meal. Note: it is so dark the hosts have to guide you to your table. After you eat each course, they'll ask you to guess what it as—it's so dark you won't be able to see it, as a rule. But a fun evening. (Don't trip!)

CHIC CABARET & RESTAURANT COSTA MUJERES
Boulevard Vialidad Paseo Mujeres Sm 3 MZ 1 Lt 10,
52 998 868 5200
https://www.palladiumhotelgroup.com
CUISINE: Dinner Theater
DRINKS: Full Bar
SERVING: Dinner, Closed Mon & Tues.
PRICE RANGE: $$$$

NEIGHBORHOOD: Quintana Roo
Located in the palladium resort/TRS hotel, Chic Cabaret offers an energetic dinner show fusing dance, music and gastronomy, all in a dimly lit romantic room. The 7-course meal and drinks (which never stop coming) are all included in one price. Reservations recommended, as space is limited. Plan on a longish evening, starting at 7:30 or so and lasting till 11. With the dinner and the show, it stretches out.

DU MEXIQUE
French
Av. Bonampak 109, esq. calle Pargo, Mz. 17, Sm. 3, Centro, Cancún, Mexico: 52-998-884-5889
www.dumexique.com/
This is one of the most unique and extraordinary dining experiences we have encountered. Du Mexique is the labor of love of Chef and Owner Alain Grimond, a master of his craft. Inside an elegant

gallery of contemporary art you will be courteously seated and given what could be the meal of your life. Don't touch the menu, which changes every day. Let Chef Grimond work his magic and choose for you a meal that you will remember forever. We are effusive in our praise, but we do not exaggerate. Guests have been moved to tears by their experience here. When your meal is over… when you have wiped the last bit ambrosia off the dessert plate and sucked it from your finger in reverent gratitude … have the coffee.

HARRY'S PRIME STEAKHOUSE AND RAW BAR
Steak, Shellfish
Blvd. Kukulcan Km. 14.2,
No.1, Cancún 17520, Mexico: 52-998-840-6550
www.harrys.com.mx
Harry's is on par with any steakhouse you'll find in the US. They serve only imported Prime USDA or Kobe beef. The service is superb. The interior of the restaurant is simply stunning. The raw bar also offers an excellent selection of oysters. When you have had your fill, fill up a little more on dessert, of which our favorite is the Key Lime Pie. Their signature touch is a complimentary portion of Cotton Candy after the meal, which we find amusing.

L'ESCARGOT
French
Calle Pina #27, SM-25 | Quintana Roo
77500, Cancún, Mexico: 52-998-887-6337
http://lescargot.restaurantwebexperts.com/

Situated in a renovated house near downtown Cancún, a mother and daughter team have created a delicious haven for food lovers. The ambience is cozy and warm, and the women give wonderful service. The food is delightful. There is an endless supply of delicious homemade bread. Our favorite dishes include the French Onion Soup and the Lamb. We also love their Patés.

LA PALAPA BELGA
European, International
Calle Quetzal No 13, Hotel Imperial
Laguna, Cancún 77500, Mexico:
52 998-883-5454
www.lapalapabelga.com
La Palapa Belga is the archetypal "hidden gem," located at the back of the Hotel Imperial Laguna. It can be a bit of a challenge to find, so we recommend taking a taxi. Once found, though you will be glad of the effort. The minimalist and rustic open-air

restaurant is uniquely situated on the mainland side of lagoon, with a breathtaking view of the Hotel Zone across the water. The food here is consistently high class. Only the best of restaurants can carry off a Duck Breast as well as here. We also recommend you indulge in the decadent Escargot. Our top pick for dessert… the Belgian Chocolate Mousse.

RESTAURANTE BENAZUZA
Blvd. Kukulcan Km 19.5, 52 998 891 500
https://oasishoteles.com/es/restaurantes/benazuza
CUISINE: Mexican
DRINKS: Full Bar
SERVING: Dinner, Closed Sunday
PRICE RANGE: $$$$
NEIGHBORHOOD: Quintana Roo
Located downstairs in the Grand Oasis Sens Hotel, this upscale eatery offers a creative menu with a strong Mexican influence. First stop is the bar, where

you get 5 creative cocktails then you're taken to your table. This is a 20-course meal ending in 3 sets of desserts. Favorites: Sea Bass and Pink Mole Duck.

RESTAURANTE CAREYES
Blvd. Kukulcan Km. 16.5, 52 998 881 7000
www.grandoasiscancunresort.com
CUISINE: Seafood/Mexican/Steakhouse
DRINKS: Full Bar
SERVING: Lunch & Dinner, Closed Thursday
PRICE RANGE: $$$$
NEIGHBORHOOD: Quintana Roo
Elegant eatery serves traditional Mexican fare with a French twist. Favorites: Bacon Filet served with a side of oyster Rockefeller and Shrimp & Fish ceviche. Dress code.

RESTAURANTE CHIANTI
HOTEL NYX CANCUN
Blvd. Kukulkan Manzana 52 Km. 11.5, 52 998 848 9300
www.chiantirestaurant.net/dine-in.html
CUISINE: Italian
DRINKS: Full Bar
SERVING: Dinner, Closed Tuesdays
PRICE RANGE: $$$$
NEIGHBORHOOD: Quintana Roo
Upscale eatery offering a creative menu of authentic Italian fare. Vegetarian options. Favorites: Pollo & Gamberoni Alla Griglia (Large boneless breast of chicken and large Gulf shrimp) and Ribeye Steak topped with rich cream sauce with shallots and green peppercorns. Excellent wine selection.

RESTAURANTE UMAMI
HOTEL NYX
Boulevard Kukulkan K.m. 11.5 Interior,
52 998 848 9300
www.nyxhotels.com
CUISINE: Japanese/Sushi
DRINKS: Full Bar
SERVING: Dinner
PRICE RANGE: $$$
NEIGHBORHOOD: Quintana Roo
Modern designed eatery offering incredible ocean views. Great sushi. Favorites: Miso soup and Sashimi. Creative cocktails.

SASI
Thai cuisine
CasaMagna Marriott Cancun Resort, Boulevard Kukulcan, Retorno Chac L-41,
Cancún 77500, Mexico: 52-998-881-2000
www.sasi-thai.com
Sasi Thai is located on the grounds of the Casa Magna Marriott. It has a wonderful ambience with seating in thatched cubicles. The service is friendly and efficient. They have the dishes you would expect from a Thai restaurant, and we really enjoy the Pad Thai. The Duck Curry is also quite tasty. We were also quite charmed with the Chocolate Tamarind Dessert.

TORA MEXICO
Blvd. Kukulcan Km. 15, 52 998 313 4128
www.toramexico.com

CUISINE: Japanese
DRINKS: Full Bar
SERVING: Lunch & Dinner
PRICE RANGE: $$$$
NEIGHBORHOOD: Quintana Roo
An upscale Japanese robata grill eatery offering traditional Japanese cuisine with a modern influence. Favorites: Ora King Salmon and Spicy Yellowtail Sushi roll. Impressive cocktail selection.

THE WHITE BOX
GRAND OASIS PALM
Blvd. Kukulcan, 52 998 881 7000
https://oasishoteles.com/en/restaurants/the-white-box
CUISINE: Seafood/Steakhouse
DRINKS: Full Bar
SERVING: Dinner, Closed Mon & Tues.
PRICE RANGE: $$$$
NEIGHBORHOOD: Quintana Roo
Fine dining inspired by a group of renowned chefs. Haute cuisine in small dishes. Great tasting menu. Favorites: Blackened prawns and Sea Bass. Impressive wine list. Only seats 20 so reservations recommended.

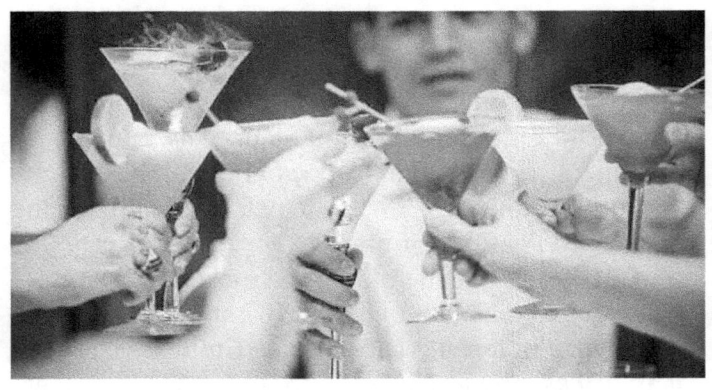

Chapter 4
NIGHTLIFE

This is a party town. All those Spring Breakers didn't come down here to gaze lovesick at the moon. They came to party, to get drunk off tequila and to dance to loud music and to get laid.

Maybe you did, too!

In El Centro, prepare yourself for music that throbs incessantly, that's loud, that's insistent.

Like any good vacation destination, Cancun is just as fun at night as it is during the day. Most of the nightclubs are located in the entertainment district at the northeast tip of the Hotel Zone. Here you can party the night away in one mega-club, or bar hop to your heart's content.

The mega-bars have made Cancun famous for its nightlife. These monster party complexes hold thousands of people. They feature a variety of acts and eye-catching visuals as well as world-class DJs.

The shows are constantly changing from moment to moment. At one moment you may be watching a contortionist, which might be followed by a bikini contest and fog machines. Internationally known performers regularly make appearances at these clubs. It is not uncommon to find such acts as Shakira or the Black-eyed Peas performing.

Coco Bongo is the oldest and most well-known of the mega-clubs, but others have come to prominence in recent years such as Bulldog, The City, Dady Rocks, and Dady O. Each of these places does its best to outdo the others, and we recommend visiting them on different nights. For those who haven't the time or stamina to visit one club a night there are nightclub tours that let you experience several of the mega-bars in one crazy night.

Drinks run $7 to $11.

It is not uncommon for the places to stay open until the sun comes up.

Here are some important tips for a safe and enjoyable night out in Cancun:

* Give your waiter a good tip up front, so they take care of you all night.

* Pay as you go, or you may be in for a big surprise.

* Keep your hands on your drink, and don't take a drink from a stranger. This goes for everybody, women and men alike.

* If you've been drinking heavily, DO NOT go home alone or try to drive a car. One thing you don't want to deal with is the Mexican police and judicial systems, pathetically corrupt as they are. Also, DO NOT travel home alone. Have someone with you or

take public transport. Don't even get into a cab alone if you can help it. You might end up in a ditch.
  * Don't leave your camera sitting around. Better yet, don't bring a camera at all.

THE CITY
Boulevard Kukulcán – KM 9.5, Zona Hotelera, Cancun, Mexico: 52-998-883-3333 ext. 138
www.thecitycancun.com
Cover runs $40-$50 (includes bar) or $25 without. Through the sprawling 3-floor and 8,000 square feet of space this huge club occupies, it's easy to get a drink – they have about 10 bars. Impressive light shows, state-of-the-art sound system, DJs imported from around the world. Though the club doesn't get started till 10:30 at night (runs till about 5 a.m.), the complex itself opens in the morning, so you can spend the day herein a cabana at the beach, by the pool. Plenty of food and drink all day and night. Different rooms offer different atmospheres. VIP Rooms. Celeb hangout.

COCO BONGO
Blvd. Kukulcan Km 9.5 Plaza Forum, Cancun, Mexico: 52-800-841-4636/ 52-998-883-5061
www.cocobongo.com/
Cover runs $50 during the week and $10 additional on weekends (includes open bar).
Many different kinds of music (salsa, hip-hop, Caribbean, techno and everything else) gets played here in one of the hottest clubs in town. (Holds over 2,500, but you'll still encounter lines). Here at CoCo Bongo, the whole place is a dance floor, from the top of the tables to the top of the bars. Famous around the world for its theme parties.

DADY'O
Boulevard Kukulcán – KM 9.5, Zona Hotelera, Cancun, Mexico: 52-998-883-3333
www.dadyocancun.com/
Cover runs about $20-$30.
Most established of the Grupo Dady cluster of clubs. Like all the big clubs here, always seeking to out-do each other, this one has a superior light & sound system. Always packed.

DADY ROCKS
Boulevard Kukulcán – KM 9.5, Cancun, Mexico: 52-52-998-883-3333
www.dadyocancun.com/
Cover runs $20-$30.
Slightly different package in this spinoff of Dady'O: here you can get pretty good Tex-Mex food, live bands, but there's still a DJ and dancing. Dining

begins at 6 p.m. on the terrace, and inside they open at 8. They have 4 bars, 2 floors, outdoor terrace, the top sound & light system, contests like Wet T Shirt, different ladies' nights, a Sexy Legs Contest (winner gets US$1500).

FORUM BY THE SEA
Paseo Kukulcán km. 9.5 zona Hotelera Cancún: 52-998-883-4425
www.forumbythesea.com.mx
WEBSITE DOWN AT PRESSTIME
Oceanfront area has it all. Here you'll find all sorts of nightlife activities: from sports bars to dance clubs, from cheapie taco stands to some of the best dining spots in the area. Lots of shopping as well.

LOBBY LOUNGE
RITZ-CARLTON
Retorno del Rey 36 | Zona Hotelera, Quintana Roo: 52-998-888-0808

www.ritzcarlton.com

For a much more subdued ambience, you'll find a small, intimate club in the Lobby Lounge in the Ritz-Carlton. It opens at 5 for drinks and light snacking, but later, there's a dance floor with a DJ. Not the young, raucous crowds you get in the big clubs. (They also offer 70 tequilas at the bar and they'll set up tequila flights for you.)

Chapter 5
ATTRACTIONS

TOURS

Everybody in Cancún has got a brother who runs a tour and they can get you a good price. Some of them really are good opportunities and others are rip-offs. We suggest you don't take any of these offers at first, and look around for a bit to get a sense of what is out there and how much it *ought* to cost. Prices fluctuate depending on the season and what conventions might be in town, so ask around. And remember, everybody is your friend when you've got money to spend.

WATER SPORTS

XEL-HA
Carretera Chetumal-Cancun km 240, Quintana Roo:
52-998-883-3143
www.xelha.com

A few miles south of Cancún is Xel-ha, which has transformed itself into a fantasy land of excitement and discovery for those who love the water and all things that live in it.

Here, you can swim with the dolphins for about $100 to $150, depending on how long you want to be in the water with them.

There are dozens of activities such as snorkeling, cliff jumping, tubing, scuba and snuba diving.

('Snuba' diving is for people who aren't certified to scuba dive. You wear a mask attached to tubes that rise to an oxygen tank floating on the surface. The tubes run around 20 feet. Quite liberating.)

They even have a devise called "Sea Trek," a large plastic piece of head gear you put on that covers your whole upper body and rests on your shoulders. You have great underwater views with this device.

The grounds are huge and feature many kinds of environments such as nature trails, cenotes, a giant lagoon, and underwater caves.

EL REY
If you are in Cancún and haven't the time or inclination to commit to a day trip to the further, more well-known sites, but still want to see Mayan ruins, then El Rey is the place for you. You don't even have to leave the city. El Rey is located at kilometer 17 in the south Hotel Zone. The bus goes right by it, and any taxi driver will know where it is.

SEA TURTLES

One of the most memorable events you can experience in Cancún is the turtle season. Cancún is home to two of the world's seven species of sea turtle – the Loggerhead and the Green Turtle. The hospitality industry on the beach is an instrumental player in the conservancy and protection of these endangered species. The laying season begins in April. Incubation lasts about two months, and the last eggs of the season hatch in October. During this season the hotels keep bright lights off the beach at night so as not to disturb the turtles, and many hotels have staff dedicated to sea turtle protection. It is very common to see turtles coming ashore to lay their eggs late at night. This is reported to the local conservancy and the eggs are quickly moved to a protected area where they can incubate in peace. When the baby turtles hatch, guests of the hotels are invited to witness the event and aid in their return to the ocean. Children and adults alike are moved by this magical experience and go home with a new insight into the need to protect the environment and all species of life on Earth.

WHALE SHARKS

The Summer months of June through September are Whale Shark season. During this time the warm waters of the Gulf of Mexico and the Caribbean Sea meet, causing an upswelling of plankton-rich water, which is a feast to these gentle giants. Whale Sharks are the largest fish in the Earth's oceans, sometimes growing to over 40 feet long and weighing over 20 tons. But don't worry, these magnificent creatures are not a threat to humans; quite the opposite, actually. During the summer months, Whale Shark tours leave Cancún daily, filled with happy tourists excited by the chance to actually swim among these giant fish.

SWIMMING WITH DOLPHINS
There are a number of dolphinariums located in Cancún, including some of the major hotels. We ask that you consider, however, avoiding these attractions. Dolphins are a highly social and intelligent creatures. They are taken from their life in the wide ocean and forced to live out an isolated existence restricted to a small, often artificial, area for the amusement of throngs of tourists. We prefer to leave our cetacean friends free in the wild.

CENOTES
One interesting fact about the Yucatán Peninsula is that there are no rivers. For various geological and

tectonic reasons, all water flows underground. The limestone rock covering reservoirs of water in many places has collapsed, leaving open-air sinkholes called Cenotes. These cenotes are often hundreds of feet deep, with crystal-clear cool water. Swimming in these cenotes is an interesting and exciting alternative to a day at the beach. We highly recommend you take at least one day to experience this uniquely Yucatecan pastime.

RUINS
It would be a shame to visit the Yucatán and not see Mayan Ruins. There are hundreds of known Mayan ruins. We list here the ones most convenient to visitors to Cancún. Take bug spray and plenty of water. And you might want to take some bananas to feed the ubiquitous iguanas.

TULUM
You've probably seen the stunning iconic pictures of a Mayan pyramid rising on a cliff above a sandy beach and turquoise waters. That's Tulum, the only significant site that was built on the ocean. Spanish sailors in the early 16th century recorded sailing by and seeing a thriving, colorful Mayan city where we now find grey ruins. The views and ambiance is stunning – our favorite, really. Tulum is located an hour and a half south of Cancún, and there are daily tours from most of the cities in the Yucatán. The site itself is not very large – one can take in the whole place in about an hour – but it is the most photogenic. We recommend arriving early in the day or later in the afternoon, for it can get quite crowded at times.

From the parking center one can take the tram for a small fee or walk the quarter mile to the site entrance. There is access to the beaches, so feel free to make a whole day of exploring the ruins then playing in the surf. The souvenir shopping center that has grown up at the parking lot is rather an eye-sore, and the prices are not good, despite what your guide will tell you.

COBA
Coba is about an hour and a half southwest of Cancún. Despite the distance, there are some good reasons to go see this site. Coba is the least restored of all the popular sites, and this gives it a wonderful Indiana Jones feel. There are many buildings that are still covered by jungle. The main pyramid is one of the largest, and visitors can still climb it and look out across the Yucatán jungle. The grounds are quite extensive, so we recommend renting bicycles at the entrance, which adds another enjoyable dimension to your excursion. Watching the crocodiles being fed in the lakes is always a thrill. There are many quaint shops along the road to Coba selling interesting tchotchkes at reasonable prices.

CHICHEN ITZA

Chichen Itza is the most popular Mayan site on the Yucatán peninsula. The site is listed as one of the Seven New Wonders of the World. It is a good distance from Cancún, but dozens of tour buses a day make the 2 ½ hour trek. We recommend having a guide for this site. Being the most famous and developed site, it is also the most restrictive. Visitors are not allowed in the buildings or to climb the pyramids. The guides provide a rich narrative to spark one's imagination and form a bond with the site. Excellent bilingual guides can be hired for a reasonable price at the entrance. Many visitors appreciate the mathematical accuracy and astrological alignment of the buildings. If possible, we recommend visiting on either the Spring or Fall Equinox, where you can join the thousands of people who come to watch the Descent of the Serpent, a shadow cast at just the right angle to create the appearance of a snake descending the Temple of Kukulcan. After a sweaty day of wandering around

Chichen Itza, we recommend you cool off with a refreshing dip in Ik Kil cenote, a few kilometers away.

ECO ADVENTURE PARKS
Recent years has seen a sharp rise in public interest in ecotourism; and the Yucatán Peninsula, with so much to offer the out-doors-minded traveler, has seen a boom in Eco Adventure Parks. Located within an hour or so of the city, these parks offer a wide range of exciting amusements from zip lines to horse riding to floating along underground rivers. Transportation is best arranged through the parks, as directions can often be vague. We recommend checking with your hotel for tickets, as they often have them at much better prices than you will find at the gate. Here are a few of our favorites.

AKTUNCHEN NATURAL PARK
Located about an hour south of Cancún, Aktun Chen offers an exciting mix of activities for all ages. The caves at this site are magical and we recommend the

tour. If above ground is your thing, go way above ground on their zip line and suspended bridges tour, which travels through the jungle canopy for over a kilometer. They also have a six-acre wildlife zoo with an emphasis on conservation. And don't miss the chance to go swimming and snorkeling in their crystal-clear cenotes.

HIDDEN WORLDS CENOTE PARK
Hidden Worlds has taken tree-top adventure to a whole new level. Besides the regular zip lines, they also have a sky cycle which visitors pedal on lines through the trees. They're big attraction, however, is a new roller coaster style zip line. Scuba diving is offered in the cenotes and there is also a zip line that drops into a cenote. Cave rappelling is an interesting adventure, and when you're tuckered out with all the physical exertion, take a relaxing ride in a jungle buggy. This attraction is about an hour and a half south of the city.

RIO SECRETO
This is one of our favorites. Located in Playa del Carmen, about an hour south of Cancún, Rio Secreto is a stunning series of caves and cenotes which will leave you speechless. There are caverns filled with so many thousands of stalactites and stalagmites that you will think you are in some surreal alien cathedral. This is a tour not to be missed.

SELVATICA
This award-winning eco theme park is closer to Cancún than most of the others, about half an hour

south. There is a wide array of zip lines, cenotes to swim in, and lots of different kinds of vehicles to bump around the jungle trails on.

XAMAN HA AVIARY

The Xaman Ha Aviary is the place to go to see the wonderful variety of bird species that populate the Yucatán Peninsula. Here you can see Snowy Egrets, Pink Flamingoes, Scarlet Macaws and Toucans, among many, many others. Located in Playa del Carmen, the aviary is much better priced that many of the other attractions in the area, and photographers are welcome to bring their equipment at no additional charge.

XCARET

Xcaret is one of the largest and oldest eco parks in the Mayan Riviera. The park features archeological sites, underground rivers, beaches, lagoons and pools, as well as educational and interactive exhibits such as aquariums and greenhouses. There are many local species of animal to interact with. In the evening shows featuring the native Mayan legends and customs bring to life the rich and vibrant history of the area.

SIAN KA'AN BIOSPHERE
The Sian Ka'an Biosphere is a leader in ecological conservation and education. Located near Tulum, the center is a model of green technology and sustainable development. A UNESCO World Heritage Site, Sian Ka'an's million acres is home to many species of rare flora and fauna and over twenty archeological sites. Those who love nature and the peace and serenity it offers will find it to their heart's content. We highly recommend renting a kayak.

Chapter 6
SHOPPING & SERVICES

SHOPPING IN CANCÚN

If you haven't already spent all your money on cenote tours and all-inclusive resorts, there is lots of shopping in Cancún as well. The Hotel Zone has several large and modern malls featuring both Mexican handicrafts and international brands. There are also the requisite chain restaurants and cinemas just as in the US. We suggest you also make the effort to get out of the Hotel Zone and go into downtown Cancún, where you can find the famous Mercado 28, as well as all the chains you know and love in the US.

PLAZA LA ISLA
Blvd. Kukulcán km 12.5, Z.H., 52-998-883-5025
www.laislacancun.com.mx

This is one of the newest and trendiest of the shopping centers in the hotel zone. On the Nichupte Lagoon, the center is built on a series of canals, with bridges connecting parts of the center, all reminiscent of Venice. There are many shops of different types, most of them pricey. Our favorite place to wander here is the souvenir emporium, where one can find some good deals. Plaza la Isla also features restaurants, a disco, and cinema.

FLAMINGO PLAZA
Boulevard Kukulkan Km 11.5, Zona Hotelera, 77500 Cancún, Quintana Roo, 52-998-883-2855
www.flamingo.com.mx
It seems that all tropical Latin-American cities have a Flamingo Plaza. Cancún's is a stylish building of marble housing designer and duty-free shops. There are also lots of Mexican arts and crafts available. Food-wise Flamingo Plaza offers many restaurants, including chains such as Margaritaville, The Outback, Pat O'Brien's and Planet Hollywood.

PLAZA CARACOL
Blvd Kukulcan Km 8.5, Z.H. 2-998-883-4760
www.plazacaracol.mx/
Plaza Caracol is the biggest mall in Cancún. It is also very modern. It is centrally located on the Hotel Zone just north of the Convention Center. There are many boutiques, including favorites such as Benetton, Gucci and Ralph Lauren. There are also some very interesting art galleries. Prices at Plaza Caracol are pretty good – certainly better that what you'd pay in the US.

PLAZA LAS AMERICAS
Av. Tulum 260, Downtown, Cancún, 52-998-887-3863
Located downtown, Cancún's version of a hometown mall has everything to make you feel at home. There are a nice assortment of local boutiques, arcades and fast-food outlets. It also features a JC Penney and a Sears.

MERCADO 28
Xel-ha Mz. 13 SM 28, 77501 Cancún, Quintana Roo, Mexico: 52-998-892-4303
www.facebook.com/Mercado28Cancun
Mercado Veintiocho. This is Cancún's most popular place to shop for souvenirs. You will enjoy wandering through the many stalls filled with bargains. Here you will find the same items offered in the Hotel Zone, but at much better prices. Haggling for a bargain is part of the fun here, so don't settle for the first price given.

INDEX

1

100% NATURAL, 31

A

AIRPORT, 6
AKTUNCHEN NATURAL PARK, 65
ALL RITMO RESORT & WATERPARK, 17
AVALON BACCARA, 18

B

BACOLI TRATORIA, 37
BEL AIR COLLECTION RESORT & SPA, 18
BLACK HOLE, 42
Blanc Spa, 19
BUS SERVICE, 7

C

CALYPSO'S GRILL AND MEXICAN FOOD, 32
CANCUN CONVENTION BUREAU, 8
CANCUN MUNICIPAL TOURISM OFFICE, 8
CENOTES, 61
CHIC CABARET & RESTAURANT COSTA MUJERES, 42
CHICHEN ITZA, 64
CITY, THE, 53
COBA, 63
COCO BONGO, 54

D

DADY ROCKS, 54
DADY'O, 54
DU MEXIQUE, 43

E

ECO ADVENTURE PARKS, 65
EL REY, 59
EL REY DEL CARIBE, 15
ELEFANTA INDIAN CUISINE, 37
EXCELLENCE RIVIERA, 22

F

FIESTA AMERICANA GRAND CORAL BEACH RESORT & SPA, 23
FLAMINGO PLAZA, 71
FORUM BY THE SEA, 55
FRED'S HOUSE & SEAFOOD, 38

G

GRAND OASIS PALM, 49
GRAND ROYAL LAGOON, 14

H

HARRY'S PRIME STEAKHOUSE AND RAW BAR, 44
HIDDEN WORLDS CENOTE PARK, 66
HOTEL DEL SOL, 14
HOTEL NYX, 48
HOTEL NYX CANCUN, 47

L

L'ESCARGOT, 44
LA HABICHUELA DOWNTOWN, 38
LA PALAPA BELGA, 45
LA TRANQUITA GRILL AND BAR, 35
LABNA, 39
LE BLANC SPA, 19
LIVE AQUA ALL-INCLUSIVE, 25
LOBBY LOUNGE, 55
LOCANDA PAOLO, 40

M

MAKI TACO, 40
MARRIOTT CASAMAGNA CANCÚN RESORT, 20
MERCADO 28, 72
MOON PALACE GOLF & SPA RESORT, 26

N

NIZUC RESORT & SPA, 20

O

OMNI CANCÚN HOTEL, 21

P

PLAZA CARACOL, 71
PLAZA LA ISLA, 70
PLAZA LAS AMERICAS, 72

R

RAMADA CANCÚN CITY, 15
Ramona, 20
RENTING A CAR, 7
RESTAURANTE BENAZUZA, 46
RESTAURANTE CAREYES, 47

RESTAURANTE CHIANTI, 47
RESTAURANTE LE NATURA, 33
RIO SECRETO, 66
RITZ-CARLTON, 23, 55
RIU PALACE LAS AMERICAS, 24
ROYAL CANCÚN, 27
RUINS, 62

S

SASI, 48
SAVIO'S BISTRO BY LA DOLCE, 41
SEA TURTLES, 60
SELVATICA, 66
SHOPPING IN CANCÚN, 70
SIAN KA'AN BIOSPHERE, 68
SOL Y LUNA, 12
SOTAVENTO HOTEL AND YACHT CLUB, 16
SUITES GABY HOTEL, 16
SUN PALACE, 26
SURFIN BURRITO, 34
SWIMMING WITH DOLPHINS, 61

T

TAXIS, 6

TEMPTATION RESORT SPA CANCÚN, 21
Terra Nostra, 20
TERRACARIBE HOTEL, 16
Timeshares, 11
TORA MEXICO, 48
Transportation, 6
TRATORIA LA VENEZIANA DA BERTILLA, 36
TULUM, 62

W

WESTIN LAGUNAMAR CANCÚN, 22
WHALE SHARKS, 60
WHITE BOX, 49

X

XAMAN HA AVIARY, 67
XBALAMQUÉ, 13
XCARET, 67
XEL-HA, 59

Z

ZOETRY PARAISO DE LA BONITA, 27

WANT 3 FREE THRILLERS?

Why, of course you do!

If you like these writers--
Vince Flynn, Brad Thor, Tom Clancy, James Patterson, David Baldacci, John Grisham, Brad Meltzer, Daniel Silva, Don DeLillo

If you like these TV series – House of Cards, Scandal, West Wing, The Good Wife, Madam Secretary, Designated Survivor

> You'll love the **unputdownable** series about Jack Houston St. Clair, with political intrigue, romance, suspense.

Besides writing travel books, I've written political thrillers for many years that have delighted hundreds of thousands of readers. I want to introduce you to my work!
Send me an email and I'll send you a link where you can

download the first 3 books in my bestselling series, absolutely FREE.

Mention **this book** when you email me.

andrewdelaplaine@mac.com